FIRST NIGHTS

Princeton Series of Contemporary Poets

Susan Stewart, *series editor*
For other titles in the Princeton Series of Contemporary Poets see page 73

FIRST NIGHTS

Poems

Niall Campbell

PRINCETON UNIVERSITY PRESS
Princeton and Oxford

Copyright © 2017 by Niall Campbell

Requests for permission to reproduce material in North America should be sent to Permissions, Princeton University Press. All other permissions requests should be sent to Bloodaxe Books.

Published by Princeton University Press, 41 William Street, Princeton, New Jersey 08540

In the United Kingdom: Princeton University Press, 6 Oxford Street, Woodstock, Oxfordshire OX20 1TR

First published in North America by Princeton University Press. A version of this text was first published in the United Kingdom under the title *Moontide* in 2014 by Bloodaxe Books Ltd.

press.princeton.edu

Jacket art: *Winter Landscape*, by Karl Hagemeister. Courtesy of Getty Images

All Rights Reserved

ISBN 978-0-691-17294-1

ISBN (pbk.) 978-0-691-17295-8

Library of Congress Control Number: 2016931464

British Library Cataloging-in-Publication Data is available

This book has been composed in Adobe Garamond Pro and ScalaSansOT

Printed on acid-free paper. ∞

Printed in the United States of America

10 9 8 7 6 5 4 3 2 1

For Catriona and Soren

Contents

Acknowledgments xi
Song 1
The Work 2
On Eriskay 3
After the Creel Fleet 4
The Tear in the Sack 5
Rodin Sculpts *The Kiss* 6
Black Water 7
The Cut 8
The Winter Home 9
"The Letter Always Arrives at Its Destination" 10
Midnight 12
The Blackbird Singer 13
The Fraud 14
Harvest 15
Grez, Near Dusk 16
The Water Carrier 17
One Day, Too Hot, I Swam to the Middle of the Stream 18
Lyrebird 19
First Nights 20
Exchange Street 21
An Eel, A Singing Bird, A Silver Coin 22
A Little Night Music 23
The Well Found Dry 24

Return, Isle of Eriskay   25

When the Whales Beached   26

Later Tasting   27

Crossing   28

For the Cold   29

Fleece   30

Dream   31

Le Penseur   32

February Morning   33

Sea Coins, Scottish Beach   34

Advice on Love, Over Whisky   35

A Danse Macabre   36

Leave, Eriskay   38

Grez   39

A Porch-Step Glossary for Smokers   40

Foxes   41

Epitaph   42

Forge   43

And This Was How It Started   44

An Island Vigil   45

Walking Song   46

An Introduction to the Gods of Scotland   47

Window, Honley   48

I Started   49

Cyprus Avenue   50

The House by the Sea, Eriskay   51

The Songs of Kirilov   52

Horseshoe Crab   53

Reading Emile Zola, Grez   54

Carpenter's Studio off Exchange Street   55

Concerning Song/Silence   56

Leave Poetry   57
Addendum   58
Island Cottage, November   59
Proof   60
Smultronstället, Glendale   61
A Sealskin Tale   62
Kid   63
Juggler   64
Winter with Soren   65
North Atlantic Drift   66
From a Letter to the Butter-Makers   67
Aesthetics, on a Side Street off Glasgow Green   68
Measuring Heat Loss in the Arctic   70
A Song for Rarity   71

Acknowledgments

ACKNOWLEDGMENTS are due to the editors of the following journals and anthologies in which some of these poems have previously appeared: *AndOtherPoems, Best British Poetry 2013, Best British Poetry 2015, Best Scottish Poems 2011, BODY, The Bow-Wow Shop, The Dark Horse, Granta, The Herald, Horizon, The Literateur, Magma, New Linear Perspectives, Northwords Now, Oxford Poetry, POEM, Poetry London, Poetry Review, The Rialto, The Red Wheelbarrow, The Salt Book of Younger Poets* and *13 Pages*. Several of the poems in this collection were previously published in a pamphlet, *After the Creel Fleet* (Happenstance, 2012).

I would like to express my gratitude to the Society of Authors for the Eric Gregory Award I received in 2011, to the Robert Louis Stevenson Fellowship (2011) on whose residency some of these poems were written, to the Arvon-Jerwood mentoring scheme (2013) for the help offered during this program, and to the Edwin Morgan Poetry Award (2014). I would also like to thank the following people for their help, support and guidance: Patience Agbabi, Alison Angell, Neil Astley, John Glenday, Andrew Jamison, Roddy Lumsden, Helena Nelson, and Susan Stewart. And thank you to my wife, Catriona McAra, and to my son.

FIRST NIGHTS

SONG

What sweeter triumph can there be
than the match lit in the grain cellar,
no moon in the dark gallery
below the sleeping house. It's better

when I'm alone—can freely handle
those older tools for harrowing
and planting, turn the bent seed-cradle,
or thumb the axe blade like a harp string.

THE WORK

If I have to, then let me be *the whaler poet*,
launcher of the knife, portioning off
the pink cut, salt trim and fat, tipping
the larger waste off the side of the boat,
and then to have the poem in the drawer;

or, perhaps, let it be *the poet nurse*,
hearts measured by a small watch, balmer,
washer of old skin, stopping by the door
in the night—
              or *the oil-driller poet*, primed
for the buried flame and heat, lips to the black,

aware how the oilfields in the evening
are lit like our own staggered desks.
Or, *the horse-trader* or *the smith*, or *the waiter poet*—
offering the choice wine, polishing to the light,
the bringer of the feast and the bill.

ON ERISKAY

She met me at the fence. A kelpie
who'd stayed too long in this horse form,
she mouthed the sugar on my palm,
and when I slapped her barrel flank
the goose moor stiffened with a sea
perfume. Gulls gathered on the stoop.

What a way to be seen out: confused
among the pearlwort and the fallow.
Her beach songs, like the recalled taste
of bucket milk, inched from her tongue.
Dusk grew behind the house. I watched
her drink the moon from a moon-filled trough.

AFTER THE CREEL FLEET

I never knew old rope could rust, could copper
in its retirement as a nest for rats.

The frayed lengths knotting into ampersands
tell of this night, and this night, and this,

spent taut between the surface and the seafloor—
the water coarsening each coiled blue fiber

and strained, one strand might snap, unleash its store
of ripples to be squandered in the dark

though thousands would remain still intertwined
and thousands do remain, but frailer now.

These hoards, attached to nothing, not seen since
the last tightrope was walked, the last man hung.

THE TEAR IN THE SACK

A nocturnal bird, say a nightjar,
cocking its head in the silence
of a few deflowering trees,
witnesses more than we do
the parallels.
              Its twin perspective;
seeing with one eye the sack-
grain spilled on the roadway dirt,
and with the other, the scattered stars,
their chance positioning in the dark.

RODIN SCULPTS *THE KISS*

There with a swung hammer is a man in love,
there's crafting, and there's breaking of squared marble.
There, the white dust and the scattered chippings
of what's fashioned out. How bare it looks,

half-made—a figure leaning in to kiss
what's not there yet, the arms encircling nothing
but a rougher offshoot of themselves. And yet
the kiss is held—as though the stone the figure

cradles receives it. Here is a strange knowledge
and a strange trust: his heart can sense the stone
heart aching in the block, his lips can taste
the mountainside that shapes into a mouth.

BLACK WATER

It's China that has, as the image of sleep,
the sleeper drinking from the night sea—
their bowl first lowered, and then raised with ocean;
a fisherman's son, I'm drawn to this.

Listening to the street's late deliveries,
I picture each one I love at this beach,
bowing intent to the work, their sand plot,
the moon adrift somewhere in their curved bay.

Here's my wife beside me, and there she is,
all lips and black water—I could ask,
where is my beach, my long sea? But, instead,
I'll raise this waking to my mouth, and drink.

THE CUT

There must at any given moment be an abstract right or wrong if any blow is to be struck; there must be something eternal if there is to be anything sudden.

G. K. CHESTERTON

    I had gone walking in the forest—not
    for any need of wood or kindling
    but rather just to feel across the shoulders
    the full weight of the question of the axe;

    the forest sounded to a hundred axmen,
    a hundred axwomen's blows—they never tired,
    it seemed, and their trees—so thick—didn't split
    or fall, at least not to my listening.

    At times, I allowed myself a dream of felling:
    the metal blade imparting its own catch
    of light into the tree's so-tender bole,
    my own bright sweat on brow and hands and back;

    ah bliss, I thought, and I swung dedicated,
    loud, against the bark of this dreamed tree
    or that. These thoughts made the route home seem short,
    and once or twice I even stopped to tap

    against the length of one that stretched or towered.
    I pressed a licked thumb to the wood. Perhaps,
    soon, I would make to start. Then, as is right,
    burn the rest of the forest to the ground.

THE WINTER HOME

Darling, allow me the best evenings
to breathe the cold, to ruminate
like a diver on his rising breath.

The low-backed seat of the house step
inches ever further from the road.
And there's the jasmine opening

in garden branches. A white flower,
unfurling in the sub degrees,
in its pale rush of residing.

"THE LETTER ALWAYS ARRIVES AT ITS DESTINATION"

—then I wrote often to the sea,
to its sunk rope and its salt bed,
to the large weed mass lipping the bay.

The small glass bottles would be lined
along the bedroom floor—ship green
or church-glass clear—such envelopes

of sea-mail. Only on the day
of sending would a note be fed
into each swollen, brittle hull—

I had my phases: for so long
it was maps: maps of wader nests,
burrows and foxes dens, maps where

nothing was in its true position—
my landscape blooming from the surf.
Later, I'd write my crushes' names

onto the paper, as a small gift.
The caps then tested and wax sealed.
None ever reached my dreamed America,

its milk-white shore, as most would sink
between the pier and the breakwater,
and I would find that I had written

about the grass to the drowned sand,
again; and to the sunken dark,
I had sent all the light I knew.

MIDNIGHT

My heart had been repeating *oh heart, poor heart*
all evening. And all because I'd held my child,
oh heart, and found that age was in my cup now;

poor heart, it bare knew anything
but the life of a young axman in the forest,
whistler, tree-feller, swinging with the wind,

where *oh heart, poor heart* isn't the heard song,
where there is no cry in the night, no cradling,
no heart grown heavy, heavier, with opening.

THE BLACKBIRD SINGER

There we were at our hidden pastime:
one lugging a box and prop, another
who stole from a farmer's store the grain
that served as bait, and then the last
who'd imitate the call of a blackbird,
flirting them out from the bush.

The sound of beating wings. Such bliss
to listen to a sprung trap—our flawed
songbox that only played when shut,
so when you lifted the wood lip
from the pressed dirt its singer bolted
like a dark adolescent thought.

Back then, we heard of those who throttled
what they trapped—whose milk hands knew
the sureness of the yellow beak,
who would, then, skirt the stiffening frames
over the deep grass, the wings bent
on journeys always straight and short.

My brothers gone off for the night,
I'd stay to dream the symmetry
housed in the act: lifting the lid
to find the same song in my hands
as in my mouth—then the same silence,
lifting from the field like a gunshot.

THE FRAUD

How like a shepherd or herdsman of loss
I must have whistled out into the evening
that a childhood dog came cowering to my heel:
years under, its coat now wool-thick with soil
and loosely collared with the roots of bog-myrtle.

A surprise, then, my old companion strained
to sneak by me to the fire and my wife.
Checked by a boot, it bore not its dog's teeth
but a long, black mouth. Then it slunk back to the hill.
Some nights I hear this thin dog claw the door.

HARVEST

I've been thinking too much about the night
I slipped and the coal scattered on the snowed drive.

Then it was time spent in luck's appleyard
gathering its black fruit; or it was time

collecting what I'd left too long to gather,
a harvest all wilt and harrowed—anyway,

it was time spent, and I held the steel bucket,
filled it to the sound of nothing at all.

GREZ, NEAR DUSK

Just a postcard to say not that it has rained
but that it smells impossibly of rain.

Moths feed on this silk hour, there's smoke from chimneys
where families are preparing for the change.

Let me explain how the bowed sky is heavy
with the deep song of the failing color

and yet it's missing. But stay. Wait with me.
Things will be different when the sun is lower.

THE WATER CARRIER

I want to be the worst of this profession,
the one who makes it home half-empty, tipping
more air than water from the ringing pot,
and so late back the town's already dark;

Oh no, they'll say, *that's not the way of it,*
and I'll know their heaven's brimful and undrunk,
their lips parched.
                    What do they know of the kiss
on the shoulder of that first spilt drop,

the tuneful drip, drip, drip on the stone path?
Midway home, midway from the source, my dream-sun
bleaching the sky, what could be better than
dry road ahead, my flooded road behind?

ONE DAY, TOO HOT, I SWAM TO THE MIDDLE OF THE STREAM

The alternative was to be the man,
ashore, who says *no, this will do*: the bulrush
and timothy, the reeds and the long braced life
of firm and flowered land;

or the alternative was to be a burning type,
and set a fire, adding one more degree
of brightness, one more degree of heat,
hoping the hours were glad of this;

or the alternative was to be the tired traveler,
my head put down on a curled-up shirt,
my hours given over, my name given up,
and not to even hear the stream;

or the alternative was not to be the swimmer,
but just the swimmer's hand, his driving on;
or just to be the swimmer's lung, filled and spent,
and not to care to where I'm calling.

LYREBIRD

Owner of no plainsong,
it had come too late
to the song box
on the first day,

the other birds
having emptied it.
What a heart, then,
or what a damn fool

to hear the axe-fall,
the backfiring car,
a world break apart
and think to sing it.

FIRST NIGHTS

Young father, is that you at the night drum,
playing soft, as though the lark was easy woken?
It's me—I didn't think there was a listener.

Then why, young father, do you play?
                                        It snows
beyond the window, the whole house sleeps—and, love,
I'm carrying something that is a change.

What do you make, young father, of the lateness,
are you a little drunken with the dark?
Yes, my head swims; I lean this head against
the solid wall, and hum to these new cares.

So, go on, tell what you hope for, young father.
Not sleep—not day, not company—just let
snow fall, light burn, glass shatter, let things slide,
let the new change be unlike the old change.

EXCHANGE STREET

Blue ambulance lights beach against the streetlamps.
What a night to depart, with the first storm
of winter still a day from breaking and the town's
palest girl due to wear that reddest dress
she wears so seldom. Just imagine,
hung on to hear, perfected, from the window,
as the sleet falls, that hush in her red wake.

AN EEL, A SINGING BIRD, A SILVER COIN

These are my favorite stories: where a sealskin
is found by the grey rockpools by the sea,

or a sickly girl, when other cures have failed,
is starved for a week—

and whoever flayed the skin was perfect:
it lifting thin but whole, dark as handled silk,

and when the week's gone, the girl sickens up
an eel, a singing bird, and a silver coin,

and soon he sleeps in it, dreaming he is
a moving sea and it his brighter surface,

and there her singing bird dies on the stones,
while her thin eel slips off beneath the door,

and now he's waist-deep in the ocean, turning
inside the current, launching his spent waves,

and since it's all that's left, the girl picks up
her silver coin, and swallows it again—

Sometimes—who'd want the comfort? Young, in love,
but it's defeat, now, that seems the good honey:

being the girl who's empty but for silver,
the man who's naked but for a coat of salt.

A LITTLE NIGHT MUSIC

I've served apprentice to a watchmaker,
who knows how long—my job to pair
the wheel-cog to its pocketcase,

or, like a servant with a young prince,
to wash the little golden hands.
I dream of springs and time, and aiming

grit at a drum of brilliant darkness:
a game that starts the evening ticking.
Bowed over clockwork, the hour's stress,

I think about the night's stretched frame
and pockets full with the day's gravel:
so much is just this bearing stones.

THE WELL FOUND DRY

Part wailed—part walked off, as though shamed
to be seen in so much want;

part licked the walls that lowered to the drop;
part, slack-jawed by the loss, chewed mud

from the well bed with a happy face;
part broke the bucket—then part sucked

the grainy panels—for the moisture left;
part blamed and called; for part there was relief;

part looked on; part looked on confused
having never cared or known of thirst.

RETURN, ISLE OF ERISKAY

Hardly a gesture at all but let me
twin the fact of the bay frozen over
with a light being in the window
of the abandoned house.

Let's talk of their comparable hush;
how, in its all-year winter, plaster
snows from abandoned walls, and gathers;
how even when this cold, the ice weeps.

WHEN THE WHALES BEACHED

On that day of spades,
engraving lines and inlets in the sand,

so that we could begin the slow
unmooring of those black shapes to the waves,

it was hard to think of anything
but how soon my grandmother

had followed her husband earthwards. Love,
and yet so much more than. The quiet

union of sometimes being the one
to lead, sometimes to follow. And these

who softly climbed the aching stair
of shore together, and didn't fall short.

How we stood by as if we'd nothing
to say, when, love, I did. I do.

LATER TASTING

Who knows what he meant by that first-last gift
of grit and pollen and sheep-dirt, and rain,
and whatever was on the hand that picked them:
diesel, linen soap, fish blood, with peat crumbs
not emptied from the picking bucket.
The berries sieved beneath the garden pump.

Now pot, now jam-sugar and upper heat
and soon the felt cream lifted off, too sweet,
too sour, for tasting.
                      Bees strike against
the kitchen glass; nectar birds turn in the air
somewhere in their lost jungles. My grandfather,
knowing what a mouth is for, watches it cool,

then asks to hold the bundle of his grandchild
and feeds this less-than-one year old, this milk child,
one teaspoon; the child shivers through the taste.

Today, I find another jar—still red
as a letter seal—and find it sweet, so sweet,
so sweet—and think I nearly understand him.

CROSSING

Say that the song was never written,
would it have settled there, I wonder,
on that far shore of the tongue's river,
singing itself, stubbing its heels
into the bank that is pure air?

Or would it wait for further passage?
Stood on the quay so long until
a form all spit and bone and light.

Am I some whistling ferryman,
trailing my pen hand in the wake?

FOR THE COLD

The last tenant of our newest house
had the gas boiler fire up in the late hours.
And so, last night, so cold, I listened to
the floorboards warp in the unwelcome heat.

I barely slept. The thought of him stretched out
beside us, hot as a hand that gives the slap.
Since then the water tenses in the pipe,
as his darkness changes to my dark.

FLEECE

Given a choice of anyone unmentioned
in literary history, I'd sink
for a while into the stock frame of the shearsman
at Colchis—when they took the ram to him.

Such craft for the hands: leavening the gold
from the pale underskin; his head right down
to the knife line, he'd hear the whispered dub-
dub of the heart locked inside its red room.

The bats flown out above our tiny house,
I want to face the stiff wool folding back
on this his one, best hour: its golden sleeve;
the knife already blunting in his hand.

DREAM

I heard him crying in his sleep,
my two-month-old—and marveled, when,
perhaps, I should have woken him;

young, young boy, already he seemed
to be drawing from his human well,
sipping the taste, learning the balance

that must be paid for his new hours:
his milk for later's bitter milk.
Who'd have known we knew this so early?

I did not wake him, though he cried,
but bent above his cot—and talked
him through his dream, until he settled.

LE PENSEUR

Perhaps I'm by the river, as the moths
for the seventh night in a week

emerge to butt the brightest windows,
the hot days gone by listening

to the rain-rhythms of the locals
and in practicing my own line,

my *je ne comprends pas*,
assured as a bronze bell, and used

so often that they rightly wonder
what it is I do understand.

So, later, drafting a thinnest gospel,
I'll versify the river and its passing,

the moths, their practice, and a bare sky.
Let them make of it what they will.

FEBRUARY MORNING

The winter light was still to hit the window,
and all my other selves were still asleep,
when, standing with this child in all our bareness,
I found that I was a ruined bridge, or one
that stood so long half-built and incomplete;

at other times I'd been a swinging gate,
a freed skiff—then his head dropped in the groove
of my neck, true as a keystone, and I fixed:
all stone and good use, two shores and one crossing.
The morning broke, I kissed his head, and stood.

SEA COINS, SCOTTISH BEACH

Like rain's own tender fossil print;
or a drowned man's blue kiss, given over
to the great swell that took him home
by its straight and coldest route.

Oxidized copper: sweet, burdened trader;
purged of its minting date, its monarch,
everything but a bluest stamp
that sets the borders of its country.

ADVICE ON LOVE, OVER WHISKY

Northerner, I say never mind
that you've stood there with a sail
and not received one kiss of wind;
and your rainwater pail

has not been touched by rain;
distil, then, in a closed barrel:
be malt, be smoke, be the threshed grain
turned dark as caramel.

A DANSE MACABRE

(a mural for Eriskay Village Hall)

    The tinker leads the way,
            tapping spoons, flourishing
    his tin-hook tin-nail bracelets,
            burnt pots loll from his belt,

    and the packman follows,
            hands flagged with penny hankies,
    two-shilling cloths—a-grin
            with death—and pat-a-patting

    the lost store of his suitcase,
            like a burst drum. Next, peddlers,
    boatmakers, farriers,
            swinging hands, fashioning

    the night into a rough step
            that leads to herring girls,
    still gutting soft parts from
            slack fish, but loosening

    their hips, as though they weren't
            now bed-promised to the sea.
    Ahead the next loud troop
            comes the horse-charmer, flanked

by foals and mares—whose dance
> is stamped into the dirt.
And last the *seanchaithe*,
> stooped man, who shakes, turns, flails

like a wind vane in the storm;
> dancing the same as all
of them: against the music,
> against the whole shamed dance.

*Packman—one who travels hawking cloths and linens; *seanchaithe*—bardic storyteller.

LEAVE, ERISKAY

I know the feeling of the grain farmer
who packed up and left his smallholding:
and not for the famine or the drought
but for the light being always on his back.

GREZ

There is the red-lit desk and wooden chair,
so now for evening's stove smoke, mothwork,
sun-in-the-leaves of the yard's birch. The quiet
that is Edith Piaf on a record player
a neighbor always lets turn at this hour—

and since that is my suitcase by the door
I'll drag it, as though it were an errant child,
to the stairwell, then the town limit, then
the short road of an empty railway platform.
There is the bending river by the hill
that I always saw—but, now, let me say
I saw it once, the hundred times the once.

A PORCH-STEP GLOSSARY FOR SMOKERS

Autumn: new-bag vanilla pipe tobacco
under the north city's long coat of rain.
My hours of connoisseurship have refined
to a series of beckonings and dismissals.

Leather and liquorice. The heavy flavors.
Then the sweet-grained and green: *scratched lime, oak barrel,*
sent jostling with their hundred other songs
and their own dark cloud, past the homes of Knightswood.

When else (when awake) will one thing hold
so many hidden names? *Grass. Rust. The summer
before the summer before the drought.* And more
to be mined out, had I the hours or breath.

FOXES

Why shouldn't they love their scavenging,
and who's to say there isn't a hard-won
joy in their distrust—of all our noise;

we pass, then they emerge, proclaiming
our wake as their live element,
but quietly so. The dim streets

do not resound for them; perhaps
a bin lid falls, but that is it.
The world isn't theirs, neither is heaven.

The littered garden opening
for them is less bright and less easy,
then they slip out of view with a shrug.

EPITAPH

(for Calum)

    The wind was carried on his voice
    to Ruban and stone pier
    and to the horses' fencing post;
    the silence didn't care

    for him, nor him for it. His church-bell
    swung out for his long life;
    only when night fell on the dark isle,
    it tolled and cracked in half.

FORGE

    There you were, farrier and blacksmith,
    who if called upon would have
    gutted the house for metals, every
    lock and moth-hinge.
                      The high tide of trade,
    the toughening and nightwork: shaping
    your dark materials—horseshoes, pins,
    those small charms we fastened at the breast.

AND THIS WAS HOW IT STARTED

The bet began when someone told the singer
he didn't know a thousand songs——
and his reply, cheered, was a ballad sung
about the foolish bet; the next praised wine,
and wine was poured and brought; and the third, sung
towards the barmaid, earned that easy kiss.

Tally was chalked against the wall. Hours followed
of step songs, dancing tunes, until at dawn
he went through every rising hymnal—where
the sun was a balanced coin, god's thumbprint on
a tipping glass—though not a thousand songs,
it was enough for us to claim him victor,

but on he went: day song, dusk song and night;
the boatmen's tunes, the spanish elegies.
He stood, a hopeful groom, through his full day
of wedding hymns: the march, the kissing waltz
and bedding. After this he sang the spade
and earth of burials, fog on his breath.

Late on the fifth day, panicked by a silence,
he clicked and whistled through the blackbird's song,
the petrel's and the wren's—and we allowed it.
And then he sang the wave-fall when there's moonlight,
sang the black grain, its bending in the wind,
then sang the stars—and then, and then, and then.

AN ISLAND VIGIL

> . . . some held that the sweetness or rankness of putrefaction gave more insight into a person's true character than hearsay or anecdotal evidence . . .
> FROM D. SIMMONS, *FOLKLORE IN PRE-REVOLUTIONARY RUSSIA* (1941)

It wasn't warmth rising from her skin
then, but the smell of weed and buttermilk;

and hers a life of lamp oil and old honey
her small hands gifted over this double scent;

and there was beach sand and beach salt,
the fruit she ran beneath cold water.

Some prayed. A candle was lit—then blown,
and all that was in the air was smoke.

WALKING SONG

I didn't know there was a crossroads
until I stumbled onto it
or that this might have a slower road
till I mis-chose and traveled it;

I couldn't bear the forest's ditch-rose,
but wore the tired head of it;
I didn't know there was a right road
until I broke and strayed from it.

AN INTRODUCTION TO THE GODS OF SCOTLAND

Aberdeen
The eyeless. The enduring. The cautious that hid his great gifts, for the greater part, out of our reach. Who prefers his churches straight and grey. He is depicted always on the rock face. He wears nothing but the grey doe-hide he skinned on the first day.

Edinburgh
In the beginning there was the stone, and this god of the rock quarry. It is tribute to him that candles and songbirds are lowered into mineshafts. Bridge builder. Castle founder. Do not look for him in the wood grain or the watermark. He reveals himself only in the grand. Moss has formed in his joints, his mouth, his eyes.

Glasgow
The god of the trafficker. She lent her tongue to the seabird, her strong arms to the haulier, her silver tongue to their customs men. Who preached her own blasphemy—if only to hear her name on many tongues. Fickle. Strange. Mother to Babel and the high-rise. Never is the rain thought to be her remorse.

Dundee
The night god. His skin pale as shell. Built up his own high church only to misplace himself. The oldest. The frail and forgetful. Each of his twelve commandments trail off. . . . By an error, he invented cannibalism. Often portrayed hunched over a star chart—trying to remember each constellation, why he had formed them, for whom.

WINDOW, HONLEY

The village bell's been broken for a month,
sounding a flat, wrecked chime to the main hour;
the clapper between its iron walls sung-out,

so I'll ask what time matters anyway:
just light, less light, and dark; the going-off
of milk or love; our tides claimed back: weed rafts,

green wood and all; those old wolves disappearing
from the bleak forest that we dream about;
a town fire; a town flood; the marriage that

left confetti in the streets until the storm;
yesterday's sweet unrust; a man with pen
at a lit window that he's long since left.

I STARTED

I started at the furthest point,
telling the road it was a lie,
and on I went. I told the wall,
the kissing gate, the swinging sign,

then told the school it was a lie;
the woman and the men that passed
I told; each rock, and word, and door.
And I did not spare my own house.

And then it rained—and I told the rain,
and told the rain that I was cold.

CYPRUS AVENUE
(for A)

You never walked
the railway sleepers,
I'm sure. Or drank
this cherry wine

that's sung about.
But on the day
you died, I heard
this song again

and thought of you
tipping it back,
draining the bottle
that couldn't be drained

and traveling this
long route—the music
stopping, a music
carrying on.

THE HOUSE BY THE SEA, ERISKAY

This is where the drowned climb to land.
For a single night when a boat goes down

soaked footprints line its cracked path
as inside they stand open-mouthed at a fire,

drying out their lungs, which hang in their chests
like sacks of black wine. Some will have stripped

down to their washed skin, and wonder
whether they are now more moon than earth—

so pale. Some worry about the passage,
others still think about the deep. All share

a terrible thirst, wringing their hands
until the seawater floods across the floor.

THE SONGS OF KIRILOV

There's no ground for resentment in all this. We've entered into a world in which these are the terms life is lived on. If you're satisfied with that, submit to them, if you're not, get out, whatever way you please.

SENECA, LETTER XCI

Kirilov was sitting on the leather sofa drinking tea, as he always was at that hour.

DOSTOEVSKY, DEMONS

Rain in the air, the smoke rose and rose smoke;
the wife of the small town's perfumer dead,
how he burns her last clothes in the garden.
Their red hours he spent redressing the air
around her. Tonight, his evening breeze,
although so painfully sweet, is still sweet.

∎

My favorite thing: to go in the storm
to a town plantation, and watch the peach trees
suffer the gale coming for their soft globes.
Sat, soaked through, pocketing the rain,
knowing for the walk home there would be bruised fruit.
Unred, unripe. Just one will fill the palm.

∎

The wolf stalked the winter forest,
its ribs a veiled fist. Tasted nothing
but the long empty plate of snow—
listening to the willow-weed,
the birch, the wind that runs through them.
Deciding just the same: that wolf
should be the last taste on a wolf's lips.

HORSESHOE CRAB

Oh son, while others
grew delicate,
these carried on,
armored and silent,

marching in their
unfollowed, unlit
torch procession
to lasting out.

Take pride in your hurt,
when the skin breaks
or the blood runs,
or when the chest

seizes and weakens;
this is the line you're from;
so come, take the match,
see how the flame burns.

READING EMILE ZOLA, GREZ

Somewhere out past the open window,
the mute's choir of thorn apple, honeysuckle,
and girls in red tops sleeping on thick grass,
face down or face to the sun—teasingly
disclosing tender shapes they would take on
in a double bed, morning splayed across them.

Imagine me here, sat watching the village
like a village's illest child at my high window.
My bookish convalescence. A lone affront
to the sure and sun-kissed, the orange tree,
the blissful, heavy pollen of a hot day,
I measure my paleness against the clouds.

CARPENTER'S STUDIO OFF EXCHANGE STREET

On the good evenings, I dream a ruined path
through dust and chipping; a hand raised to the plane
on the near wall. Strip timber will be thinned
at the long bench to something even light
could serve as prop to—task, please visit me;
this is the work, this is no work at all.

CONCERNING SONG/SILENCE

Do you remember when he wrote
his weathered book of joy—and out

went the desk lights above our own
thin books, all wick and taper smoke,

and at no loss. For a moment it
was simple: an ink house, an ink

tree, blown to leaf, and the strange bird,
joy, shivering in the inked gorse.

Then, the head gathered some of what
the heart already knew of quiet:

the hush, the burr, the meadow-weed,
that this is all, and this enough.

LEAVE POETRY

(after Luis Muñoz)

for those who are diminished or half-formed.
for those rare, unnamed birds on the bird-table.
for those who want to leave, but never do.
for those who talk, sing, curse, all without speaking.
for those who are alone.
for those who never share their evenings between two.
for those who, like mules, prefer the burden
and the journey through the unmapped provinces
of painful years, and don't search for their youth.

Leave poetry

for when you need the guide of its magnetic north.
for the nights you wake, your throat too dry
for prayer, it can be your water.
for times you need a second, imagined life,
or times you wish to sleep a restless sleep.
because it watches us even until death
with its unflickering eye, and open mouth
that sings of nothing but beauty.
for it gives us no explanations:
and this is sufficient,
and this is insufficient.
Leave poetry, my friend, for the shadows that retreat at morning.

ADDENDUM

Do you recall how I told you of the woods
outside the French town: moth-heavy, a perfume

of sackcloth emanating from the scrub.
I add to this the dark bloom of a life

discovered, pursed and fat, beside the slope.
How I wish I'd cut it from the branch.

ISLAND COTTAGE, NOVEMBER

Those nights, our lantern oil reflected
the only star of the lantern light

as we lent shadows to the walls
of our rented house. Then, I walked

into our bedroom and found her
unplaiting her hair. That night it snowed.

Now I'll retell the evenings, plain
and spare, as though a parable

of things come right. Developing
a moral in the white fall of snow,

our exhaustible form of light,
those borrowed rooms we'd made our own.

PROOF

Maybe you've heard
the drummers' test,
their one for fame,
starts with the unpeeling

of the skin or hide
from the drum frame;
and that it ends
with the straight hand

against the tenser air,
and the production
of a sound that
the ears, the lips,

and hands might claim
was the exact same sound
as before—

SMULTRONSTÄLLET, GLENDALE

Will all this—ram's wool flagged on a neighbor's fence,
ash-ruined grates, the wind-sprung thatch and gravel—
soon be recalled as wild strawberries were,
rain-fattened, fast along his childhood's verge?
Something halts, hangs, stalls over those small hearts,
near lost, in long weeds; reaches out for them.

A SEALSKIN TALE
My Version

This time there is no rockpooled shore,
no sealskin and no sealskin girl,
and never will the man make strides
across the sands that are not there.

This time, the story has not changed
despite there being no harr or thatch
or bracken—no strand, no wedding bed
for skin or shadows to lie on.

In fact, this time, there is no sun
to rise on anything, there's just
the sea and just the dark. I do
not know what story this is telling.

KID

This is it, the true time, when little matters;
when the sun's dropped so low behind the hill
that the light fails, and doesn't mind its failing;

and art is just the kid by a now pink river
kicking stones out to midstream. Hey kid, dreamer,
here's a road and a tune, just whistle out

to dusk-fall—sometimes, the song carries; sometimes,
the shadow casts out longer than the man.

JUGGLER

    I know the thing the apple passes through
    between its peak and catch:
                          and the small grace
    short-held in the collecting palm
    and why the fruit must not be eaten later,

    and I know the trembling and the risk,
    the pardoning for stray light, gusts, the audience,
    and know the pact: that my hands finish
    filled or empty—with neither feeling right.

WINTER WITH SOREN

How good to watch him sitting there,
herding his model animals
as he builds himself a little soul;

his cattle are all ranked and silent,
he tips their whole, light bodies when
he makes for them to eat or drink,

so unaware he'll not just have
the one—for lasting out—a soul
to spend years building at, all ocean,

all January sun, streaming cold,
all winter honey, all cracked stone.
Then one day it just isn't right,

the inner shape blown out, so he
must set to making something different;
his chest will hurt, how could it not,

but he must start again—like this:
with a space and a thing to care about,
with animals all bellowing,

while being guided to their pen;
my new soul, today, is a palmed toy
that longs to hear the click of a gate,
not caring if it opens again.

NORTH ATLANTIC DRIFT

We lay together in a run bath
and thought over the rowing boat
that neither one was rowing,

the evening berthed at the bath side
with its vowel song and habit
of staying with us for a while.

The low hall light behind us,
implied only where her breast,
her hip, undressed from the water.

That night the usual swell and drift
delivered my old spoilt thought
of whether a life like this is long

or long remembered—the shirts
receding in the corner shadows
dropped as weights, or anchorage.

FROM A LETTER TO THE BUTTER-MAKERS

I just don't care about the churning cask,
I'm sorry. Or the butter loosening
to buttermilk. The work is lost on me.

What I want to know is: whether you
think of time passing as a type of spoiling,
is love, when you think of it, a hot knife;

I wonder how this work-life changes us,
to firemen is desire still a form of burning
even after stepping into a smoking house;

can the good pupil ever leave the classroom,
or do they sit through day on day of lessons:
this tutor, awkwardness; this tutor, lust.

My first job was to grade the new caught shellfish;
I'd separate those *big as a fist or heart*—
the rest thrown back. I did it for two years,
then I did it for the rest of my life.

AESTHETICS, ON A SIDE STREET OFF GLASGOW GREEN

The sky is starred by the shells of the Boches
The marvelous forest where I live is giving a ball
>   APOLLINAIRE, "LA NUIT D'AVRIL 1915"

    I will only be happy when I've withdrawn
    at least a small way, to the Trongate
    or to Watson Street, where the air, too,
    stiffens with the influence of frost.

    Glasgow shivers through its autumn mist
    that knots with the fuse smoke of bonfire night.
    Here the jacketed warm the underdressed,

    shuffle between one spot beneath the dark
    and another, waiting for the lights to begin;
    while a girl somewhere is weeping in the crowd.

    It's Apollinaire who's recalled saying *War*
    is a decidedly beautiful thing,
    but then what's not, so far removed and holding
    to the outskirts of everything: a bystander

to the blue noise of white vans passing by,
and those long shadows kissing at the wall.
Fireworks are sent into the air, fall over

the marvelous forest of the awed crowd,
and a girl with her head in her tiny hands.
The red sky doesn't mind if I say this.

MEASURING HEAT LOSS IN THE ARCTIC

When that strange camera showed how
the red coal hissing in the snow,
and the boiled water, left to stand,
were just things of decreasing brightness

on an otherwise dark screen,
we knew, then, how our one concern
was not the cold—but light. Just light
such as is trapped inside a glass

until it's filled, or such that breaks,
iridescent, if only for
a while, on the skin of the sea.
It was a peaceful sort of work

to watch as things went cooling out:
the dulling coal, the dimming water;
the man or woman who then stripped
right there to nothing—or, as shown,

right down to standing light. Forgetting
about the heat, the loss, we watched
it shake—still something of a man,
still something of a woman, but

also something of a burning tree,
upright and blazing, and more, something
of the clear glass between the curtains
when it is bright, but late, but bright.

A SONG FOR RARITY

(for E and A)

    May you find pearlriver blooming
    in your garden; and the evening-song fish
    wrestling in your net; may thatch gulls
    scatter like dice across the beach
    at you and your partner's approach;
    may your bed be made of blood oak,
    and may you love well; may stonewater
    fill your glass, and taste better than it should.

Princeton Series of Contemporary Poets

An Alternative to Speech, David Lehman
And, Debora Greger
An Apology for Loving the Old Hymns, Jordan Smith
Armenian Papers: Poems 1954–1984, Harry Mathews
At Lake Scugog: Poems, Troy Jollimore
Before Recollection, Ann Lauterbach
Blessing, Christopher J. Corkery
Boleros, Jay Wright
Carnations: Poems, Anthony Carelli
The Double Witness: Poems, 1970–1976, Ben Belitt
A Drink at the Mirage, Michael J. Rosen
The Eternal City: Poems, Kathleen Graber
The Expectations of Light, Pattiann Rogers
An Explanation of America, Robert Pinsky
First Nights, Niall Campbell
For Louis Pasteur, Edgar Bowers
A Glossary of Chickens: Poems, Gary J. Whitehead
Grace Period, Gary Miranda
Hybrids of Plants and of Ghosts, Jorie Graham
In the Absence of Horses, Vicki Hearne
The Late Wisconsin Spring, John Koethe
Listeners at the Breathing Place, Gary Miranda
Movable Islands: Poems, Debora Greger
The New World, Frederick Turner
Night Talk and Other Poems, Richard Pevear
The 1002nd Night, Debora Greger
Operation Memory, David Lehman
Pass It On, Rachel Hadas
Poems, Alvin Feinman
The Power to Change Geography, Diana O'Hehir
Reservations: Poems, James Richardson
Returning Your Call: Poems, Leonard Nathan
River Writing: An Eno Journal, James Applewhite
The Ruined Elegance: Poems, Fiona Sze-Lorrain
Sadness and Happiness: Poems, Robert Pinsky
Scaffolding, Eléna Rivera
Selected Poems, Jay Wright
Shores and Headlands, Emily Grosholz
Signs and Wonders: Poems, Carl Dennis

Syllabus of Errors: Poems, Troy Jollimore
The Tradition, Albert F. Moritz
The Two Yvonnes: Poems, Jessica Greenbaum
Visiting Rites, Phyllis Janowitz
Walking Four Ways in the Wind, John Allman
Wall to Wall Speaks, David Mus
A Wandering Island, Karl Kirchwey
The Way Down, John Burt
Whinny Moor Crossing, Judith Moffett
A Woman Under the Surface: Poems and Prose Poems, Alicia Ostriker
Yellow Stars and Ice, Susan Stewart